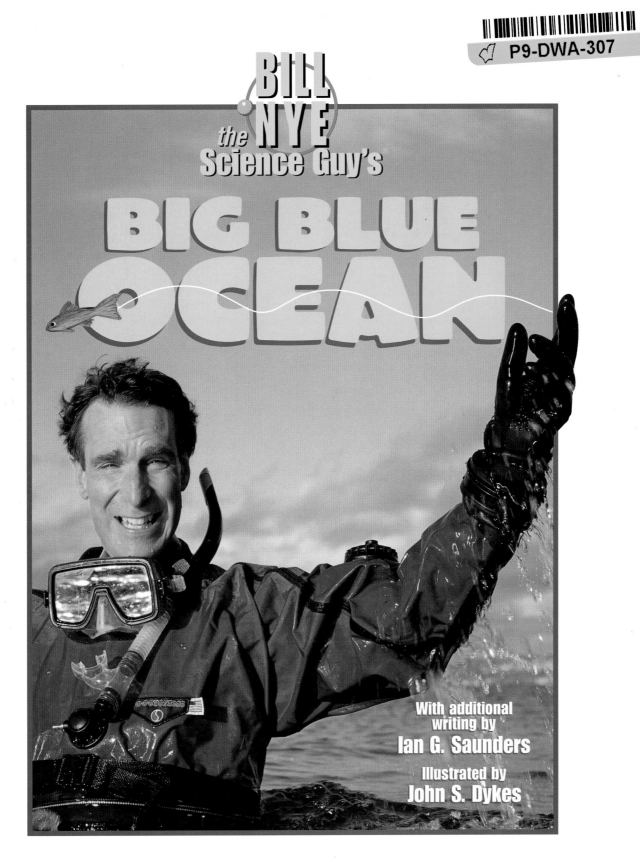

BILL NYE the Science Guy's

BIG BLUE OCEAN

With additional writing by
Ian G. Saunders

Illustrated by
John S. Dykes

Hyperion Paperbacks for Children • New York

Part of the Big Blue Ocean is for my parents; they took me to the ocean often.
Part is for Nathaniel Bowditch; he knew the science of the sea. Often I've stood
on shore or on deck and wondered what all those Earthlings are doing there;
here's hoping you do too.
—B. N.

To my wife, Alissa Kozuh, for her loving and boundless support
—I. S.

For Mom, Dad, Patti, Jeffrey, and Gregory
—J. S. D.

Text copyright © 1999 by Bill Nye
Illustrations copyright © 1999 by John Dykes
Cover and book design by Angela Corbo Gier
All Bill Nye photos by Rex Rystedt; pgs. 8–10 border © 1999 by Joshua Singer; p. 9: coelocanth © 1999 by Mark V. Erdmann;
mudskipper © 1999 by Sunset (Brake)/Peter Arnold, Inc.; eel © 1995 by Gail Shumway/FPG International LLC; guitarfish © 1999
by Marilyn Kazmers/Peter Arnold, Inc.; p. 10: all fish on bottom © 1999 by Joshua Singer; pgs. 12–14 border © 1999 by
Jeffry W. Meyers/FPG International LLC; p. 14: evisceration © 1999 by Mark V. Erdmann; p. 22: border © 1999 by
Joshua Singer; p. 48: border by Rex Rystedt

First Hyperion Paperback edition, 2003
3 5 7 9 10 8 6 4 2
Manufactured in China by South China Printing Company

Library of Congress Cataloging-in-Publication Data
Nye, Bill.
Bill Nye the science guy's big blue ocean/Bill Nye;
with additional writing by Ian G. Saunders.—1st ed.
p.   cm.
Summary: Describes the ocean and its life forms and suggests
related activities to help understand marine biology.
ISBN 0-7868-4221-0 (Tr. ed.) 0-7868-1757-7 (Pbk. ed.)

1. Oceanography—Juvenile literature. 2. Oceanography—Study and teaching—Activity programs—Juvenile literature.
3. Ocean—Juvenile literature. [1. Ocean. 2. Oceanography. 3. Marine animals.] I. Saunders, Ian. II. Title.
QC21.5.N94 1999 551.46—dc21 98-33744
Visit www.hyperionchildrensbooks.com

Science R

CONTENTS

Introducing the BIG, Wide Ocean!

Next time you're in outer space, look down at your home planet. Or just look at a picture of Earth from space . . . it's blue. It's mostly ocean—liquid water—71 percent of our planet's surface is part of an ocean. And it's the ocean that keeps our planet full of life. All the other planets in our Solar System are either too far from or too close to the Sun to have oceans like ours.

Ocean water evaporates and becomes almost all the rain that falls everywhere on Earth. That's what lets plants and animals grow. Without the ocean, ours would be a bare, and probably lifeless, world.

The Seven Seas. You may have heard the expression "the Seven Seas," but that's really from a different time, before people had sailed all the way around the world. All of the oceans are connected. So if you look at the world one way, there's just one ocean. If you look at it another way, you could say there are four: the Pacific, the Atlantic, the Indian, and the Arctic Oceans.

The water in the ocean is the same water that Cleopatra sailed and that dinosaurs drank. It's the same water that filled the first cavepeople's swimming pool! Water in the ocean today is the same water that's been on Earth since the ocean was formed over 4 billion years ago.

It's a Big Secret. We can explore the deepest reaches of outer space—places millions of kilometers away—with a telescope from our backyard. But exploring the ocean is much more difficult. We need special equipment that can handle enormous pressures and corrosive chemicals. That's why the sea still holds most of its secrets.

The Ocean Is the Most Populated Place on Earth

Up high and shallow, or down low and deep, everywhere you go in the ocean you find living things. And fish aren't the only things out there. Birds (like penguins), reptiles (like sea turtles), mammals (like whales), not to mention tons of animals without backbones, called "invertebrates" [in-VERT-uh-brits] (like squid), and tons and tons of plants (like seaweed) all depend on the ocean to survive.

If you could weigh all the living things in the ocean and all the living things on land, the ocean life would weigh a thousand times as much as the living things on land. Look around and imagine a thousand times more life. For every person, tree, and mosquito you see, think of a thousand more. The ocean is where most earthlings live.

An Ocean Desert. The moving water of the ocean makes some parts of the ocean have way more life than others. There are "deserts" in the sea, like ones found off the coast of Chile, in South America, where there are relatively few living things. Other places in the ocean, like Australia's Great Barrier Reef, have more living things on and over every patch of sea floor than on and over every patch of ground in a tropical rain forest.

TRY THIS!

THE QUESTION:
How much of the Earth's surface is covered with water?

HERE'S WHAT YOU NEED:
a basketball • a roll of 2.5-cm-wide (1 inch) masking tape (preferably blue) • a friend

1 Find a basketball and a roll of masking tape. Blue masking tape might remind you of the blue ocean.

2 Measure out 517 centimeters (203 inches) of tape. It's pretty long. You can tear it any way you like as you measure.

3 Now stick the tape on the basketball without letting it overlap anywhere. You've covered the ball with as much tape as the Earth is covered with water. Try playing catch without touching the tape. We live on a very wet world.

That's a lot of water compared to land on Earth, isn't it?

What Makes a Fish a Fish?

Like us humans, fish have skeletons, complete with a backbone. Other sea creatures, like crabs and shrimp, have no backbone, so we don't call them fish. Unlike you, fish have gills to breathe underwater. Next time you're wondering if something's a fish, use this. . . .

HANDY FISH-OR-NOT CHECKLIST OF SCIENCE:

YES NO
[✔] [ ] Does he or she have a backbone?

YES NO
[✔] [ ] Does he or she have gills?

If it's yes to both questions, then you're looking at a fish. (Unless it's an amphibian. For example, tadpoles start out with gills. Then they become frogs and grow arms, legs, and lungs.)

Smart Fish. Sometimes fish hang out together. Tuna swim together in groups of about twenty. Herring, another type of fish, travel in groups of hundreds of millions. We call a group of fish a "school." With all those fish watching out for each other and moving all the time, every fish in the school stands a better chance of surviving. See, schooling is smart for all kinds of species!

The Living Fossil

In 1939, people fishing off the coast of South Africa caught a fish none of them had ever seen before. Two meters (6 feet) long and bright blue, with odd lumps on either side of its tail fin, the fish was a coelacanth [SEE-luh-kanth]. They were thought to have become extinct in the days of the dinosaurs. Since we now know where to look, scientists and curious fishermen have caught and photographed lots of coelacanths. In fact, so many have been caught now, that they may become an endangered species after hanging out on Earth for over 65 million years!

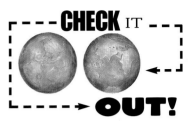

CHECK IT → OUT!

Scientists have caught up with more than twenty thousand kinds of fish, and we figure there may be tens of thousands more swimming around out there. It would take more than a lifetime just to see one of every known type of fish living in the ocean.

more REAL LIFE *fish tales*

I can leave the ocean for hours and climb trees.

mudskipper

Some of us have lived to a ripe old eighty-eight years of age.

eel
(I'm another type of fish.)

I have spines tipped with a venom as deadly as a rattlesnake's.

guitarfish?
(nah . . . just kidding)

guitarfish (no kidding!)

Fish Can Drown!

Humans can't breathe underwater. We use our lungs to get oxygen from the air we breathe, and the oxygen keeps us alive. Fish need oxygen, too. They get it out of the water using special organs called "gills." Each gill is a feathery membrane full of blood vessels. Gills move oxygen into a fish's blood the same way lungs move oxygen into our blood. Some gills are exposed, like a shark's. As a shark swims, water gets pumped through its gills. Other fish cover their gills with a hard plate called an operculum [oh-PERK-yoo-lum]. An operculum protects a fish's breathing apparatus.

CHECK IT **OUT!**

Just because fish have gills doesn't mean they don't need oxygen. If the water doesn't have enough oxygen in it, the fish can't survive. That's why fish tanks have pumps that bubble oxygen into the water.

All fish have gills. This includes the . . .

alligatorfish	crocodilefish	goosefish	parrotfish	tigerfish
birdfish	dogfish	hawkfish	porcupinefish	toadfish
boarfish	elephantfish	horsefish	rabbitfish	viperfish
buffalofish	frogfish	lionfish	sheepfish	wolffish
catfish	goatfish	lizardfish	squirrelfish	zebrafish

As you can see, there's a zoo full of gill-heads named after other animals. Some fish have even been named after other sea animals, like the whale shark. So far, we don't call any fish a fishfish. Hmm.

JUST TO SHOW A FEW

lionfish

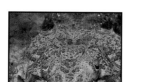
crocodilefish

hawkfish

TRY THIS!

THE QUESTION:

How can we see the gases in water that fish need to breathe?

HERE'S WHAT YOU NEED:

an unopened bottle of soda • a balloon

1 Carefully fit a balloon all the way over a soda bottle that still has the cap on.

2 Keeping the balloon on with your fingers, unscrew the cap.

Bubbles of carbon dioxide gas will come out of the liquid and get captured by the balloon. Please note that there is more gas in a liter of soda than in a liter of seawater, because the soda bottle holds the soda under higher pressure than the atmosphere holds the surface of the sea.

Gases can be dissolved in water. We can't see them, but fish can breathe them.

By the way, the sea has all kinds of gases dissolved in it, like oxygen.
(That's the gas that fish breathe.)

SEA JELLIES

Animals Formerly Known as Jellyfish

Sea jellies are not fish. Remember, a fish has gills and a backbone. A sea jelly has gills, but no bones. Sea jellies are like round spoonfuls of jam. Of course, sometimes the spoonfuls are as big as manhole covers. They're mostly mesoglea [MEZZ-uh-glee-uh]—middle glue. Most sea jellies trail long, stinging tentacles below their bodies. Any animal that gets caught in the venomous sticky tentacles becomes lunch. A group of fish is called a "school"; a group of sea jellies is called a "smack."

animal + no backbone = invertebrate

Invertebrates. We call animals like sea jellies "invertebrates" [in-VERT-uh-brits], which means "no backbone." Other invertebrates, like octopuses (or octopi), squid, sea stars, sea pens, sea anemones, [uh-NEMM-uh-neez] and sea cucumbers, live all over in the ocean. Without bones or teeth, invertebrates have evolved special ways to survive in an ocean full of predators.

The Invertebrate Hall of Fame

SEA CUCUMBER

SQUID

SEA ANEMONE

OCTOPUS

SEA STAR

SEA JELLY

Invasion of the Head-foots. Squid and octopi are closely related to snails and clams. Even though they don't have a hard covering to protect themselves, they more than make up for it with muscular tentacles and deadly venoms. Plus, they can swim away from danger in a flash—well, in a cloud of ink. Long, thin squids squirt long, thin ink clouds. Short, wide ones squirt short, wide clouds. It's to fool a foe. Because their tentacles make up most of their body, and the rest of it is head, we call squid and octopi "cephalopods," [SEFF-uh-luh-Pahdz] a Greek word that means "head-foot."

When you see a sea star, it seems like it's sitting still, but sea stars really get around. We used to call sea stars "starfish." But they're not fish—no backbones. Some move at a rate of 10 centimeters (4 inches) a minute. Others travel about 3 nautical miles (3½ miles) a month! Some sea stars team up in a big ball and roll along the bottom. When they smell a clam bed, the ball flies apart. The sea stars force clamshells open and eat the meat inside.

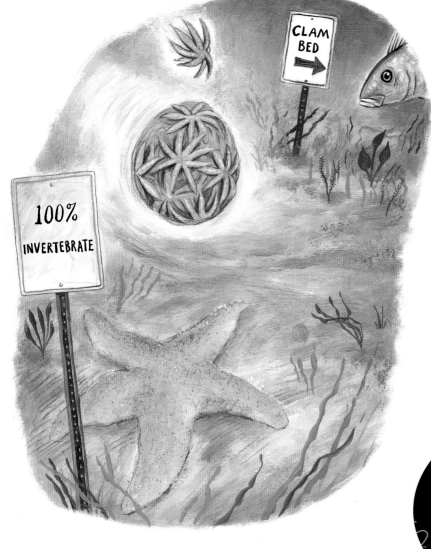

A sea cucumber feeds like a vacuum cleaner. To eat, they scoop up mud and lick tiny pieces of food off their finger-like tentacles. Sea cucumbers eat all the time. They can also spew their guts out to scare predators away. This behavior is called "evisceration" [eh-VISS-er-Ay-shun]. Sea cucumbers grow back new insides later on.

Evisceration in Action!

By the way, humans can't do this.

TRY THIS!

THE QUESTION:

How do squids defend themselves?

HERE'S WHAT YOU NEED:

handy squid reference of science • a clear bowl • water • food coloring

1 Draw a squid.

2 Fill a clear glass bowl with water.

3 Put your drawing underneath the bowl so you can see it through the water.

4 Now see how easy it is to squirt a cloud of food coloring that has the same shape.

It's not so easy, is it? But squids do it all the time.

Handy Squid Reference of Science

Be ready to dump the bowl out and start over. It's the kind of experiment that's perfect for your food preparation lab (your kitchen).

It's a Jungle Down There!

The ocean is like a jungle, where there are all kinds of food for all kinds of creatures. Mostly, large sea creatures eat smaller ones. For example, orcas eat seals. Seals, in turn, eat salmon. Salmon eat herring. Herring feed on the tiny plants and animals (plankton) that live near the surface of the ocean. We call this relationship a "food web." Each living thing in the web is connected to the other living things. There are millions of creatures that make up the huge, complex ocean food web.

There are vegetarian fish that eat plants. They're herbivores—plant eaters. Then there are fish that eat only meat, like the great white shark. They're carnivores. And there are even fish like us—that eat plants and other animals. We call these fish omnivores, which means "eats everything."

Surfing Tip of Science: Next time you hang ten, try not to look or splash like a seal. It may be that sometimes the silhouette of a surfer on a board looks like a tasty seal to a shark. Mmmmmm, yummy.

A Ferocious Hunter. The biggest carnivorous fish is the great white shark. It has several rows of sharp teeth that it uses to capture and tear into prey. Great whites usually attack from below. In the whole world, only about a dozen people die from shark attacks every year because sharks normally hunt ocean animals like seals, sea lions, or large fish.

CHECK IT OUT!

Many fish find food by using their sense of smell. When scientists plugged the nostrils of catfish, the fish couldn't find food, even when they were looking right at it.

TRY THIS!

THE QUESTION:

How much stronger is a shark's sense of smell than a human's?

HERE'S WHAT YOU NEED:

microwave popcorn (or just a paper bag with unpopped corn kernels in it) • a gym with bleachers • a microwave an extension cord • a friend • a watch

1 Place a microwave in the middle of the gym and plug it in (you will probably need an extension cord to do this).

2 Have your friend sit down on the floor about 3 meters (10 feet) from the microwave.

3 Pop the popcorn.

4 Walk up to the last bleacher and sit down on it.

5 Time how long it takes for your friend to smell the popcorn.

6 Now time how long the smell takes to reach you.

Just think, a shark can smell from a hundred bleachers farther away than you can!

SEA PLANTS

Seaweed is not a weed. Certain sea plants are like sea trees growing together in a sea forest. They're big and beautiful. They're called kelp plants. Sometimes we call all kinds of sea plants "seaweed," probably because some kinds can tangle boat propellers and swimmers' arms. But they're not really weeds. They're lovely and vital. Ocean plants, like plants on land, convert sunlight and water into the oxygen that animals breathe. And ocean plants provide a rich source of food for all the creatures in the sea. Without sea plants, animals in the ocean would have nothing to breathe and nothing to eat.

CHECK IT

OUT!

You might have eaten some seaweed today and not even known it. Certain kinds of kelp are used in ice cream, candy bars, and salad dressing recipes.

Most Earthlings Eat Plankton

Plankton is what we call the mass of all the tiny plants and animals that live in the sea. They're usually too small to see with just our eyes. Plankton comes from the Greek word for "drifter" or "wanderer." Sometimes we use the word "plankter" for one animal or one plant that drifts as part of the plankton. And that's what members of the plankton do. They drift with the ocean's currents. More than 90 percent of living things in the sea are members of the plankton. Fish and other animals eat plankton. Then larger animals eat the smaller animals. Without plankton, just about every creature in the ocean food web would disappear.

Ahhhh... Seaweed isn't the only kind of plant in the ocean. There are quadrillions of tiny phytoplankton [FIE-tuh-plank-tun] drifting in the sea, too. They're like microscopic seaweed. These plants make so much oxygen that about a third of the oxygen you breathe probably comes from phytoplankton. Weird, huh?

All the animals that swim on their own are grouped together and called the "nekton" [NEK-tahn]—the swimmers. The creatures that live on the bottom are called the "benthon" [BENN-thahn].

ICE CREAM

19

Some whales have long plates in their mouths made of a special material called "baleen" **[bay-LEEN]**, which feels like very thick fingernails. They use baleen plates like giant strainers, trapping small shrimp called krill and other plankters in their mouths while forcing seawater out with their tongues. By swimming and straining with its baleen plates, a whale eats tons of plankton. A blue whale is the largest animal on Earth. He or she consumes about 4 tons of krill every single day. That would be like eating 16,000 plates of spaghetti every 24 hours. Some scientists think that plankton will become a common source of food for humans in the twenty-first century. Whew!

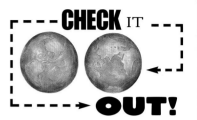

CHECK IT OUT!

In 1950, Thor Heyerdahl, a Norwegian explorer, sailed across the Pacific Ocean on a balsa-wood raft. Along the way, his crew trolled with a fine silk net. The net strained plankton from the sea, like a whale's baleen, and then the crew made soup with it. Someday, maybe you'll munch on a "McPlank" sandwich. Mmmm.

Plant Plankton

The phytoplankton are plants too small to see with just your eyes. Like miniature blades of grass, phtyoplankters live near the surface and soak up the Sun.

Animal Plankton

The zooplankton **[ZOH-uh-plank-tun]** are microscopic animals. They graze on phytoplankton and hunt each other.

TRY THIS!

THE QUESTION:

How much would a human have to eat if he/she was a whale?

HERE'S WHAT YOU NEED:

a scale • a typical lunch • peas

1 Take a scale. On one side, put everything that you would eat for lunch (for example, a peanut butter sandwich, a bag of pretzels, and an apple).

2 On the other side, pile up as many peas as it takes to balance out your meal.

If you were a whale, in a way, that's how much plankton you would have to eat to have lunch! If you can, try balancing everything you have to eat all day with peas.

Today the part of the plankton will be played by the peas.

PRETZELS

Peas of science

21

Reef
Sweet Reef

A coral reef is made by tiny coral-making animals called polyps [PAHL-ips]. They take a mineral called calcium carbonate right out of the water and secrete it as a hard, protective, cup-shaped skeleton. We call the colonies of stuck together chalk cups coral reefs. The Great Barrier Reef, off the northeast coast of Australia, stretches 2,000 kilometers (1,250 miles). It's the largest coral structure on Earth. Sea urchins, sea stars, clams, crabs, and one-third of all the world's species of fish live in and around coral reefs.

At first, a coral reef doesn't seem to have many plants. But if you look closely, you'll find tiny plants, zooxanthellae [ZOH-uh-Zan-thell-ee], actually living in the tissues of the coral animals, the polyps. At night, the polyps use their tiny tentacles and stinging cells to capture zooplankton from the water around them just like tiny sea anemones. During the day, the polyps's tentacles contract and let the cells in their bodies with the zooxanthellae inside make food from sunlight. Coral reefs are built out of chalk dissolved in the sea by tiny animals with tiny plants living inside them!

The polyps, zooxanthellae, and skeletons are all needed to make a coral reef. It is a special ecosystem with a delicate balance of temperature, wave action, sunlight, and chemicals in the sea.

CHECK IT **OUT!**

All the plankton in a coral reef typically weighs three times as much as the coral itself.

TRY THIS!

THE QUESTION:

How does sunlight affect coral reefs?

HERE'S WHAT YOU NEED:

seeds • a lamp • potting soil • 2 small flowerpots or
empty film canisters • a lamp • a table • 2 or 3 books
a plastic bag big enough to fit around the books • a shoe box

1 Plant seeds (I'm kooky for cabbage seeds!) in two separate little pots. Film canisters with good soil and a little water work great.

2 Place the plants under a light. Prop one up with books, on top of a table, so that it gets very close to the light. (If you put the books in a plastic bag, they won't get wet.) Put the other one on the floor on a shoebox, so that it's less likely to get kicked.

3 Water them now and then.

4 Watch them grow for a week or two.

> The plant that is closer to the light will grow faster, just like the phytoplankton that corals depend on. The closer they grow to the sea's surface, the more light they get from the Sun. So the coral skeletons farther from the surface get abandoned as new coral animals grow above them.

23

The OCEAN Holds the Salt!

For billions of years, salt has washed into the ocean. When the Earth first formed, it was a mass of hot rock, like lava from a volcano. There were no living things, no video games, and no oceans. The Earth was probably completely covered with clouds. Any rain that fell on the ground would have heated up immediately and turned to steam. After millions of years, the surface of our planet cooled into a hard crust. The rains created the ocean. It probably rained for thousands of years without stopping. And as water ran downhill over the land, it carried bits of minerals with it, including salt. Once salt gets carried from land to the ocean, it's stuck. Salt's got nowhere else to go.

So Much Salt. On average, the ocean is 35 parts salt per 1,000 parts water. For every 1-liter soda bottle of seawater, there's $1^1/_2$ tablespoons (35 grams) of salt.

In places that don't get a lot of rain, like the Middle East, scientists have come up with ways to take the salt out of seawater. Sometimes we boil the seawater, and cool it back to a liquid. Water from vapor has no salt. Or we pump seawater through special membranes that hold salt back like a filter. Either way, we can "desalinate" [dee-SAL-in-ate] water from the ocean and drink it.

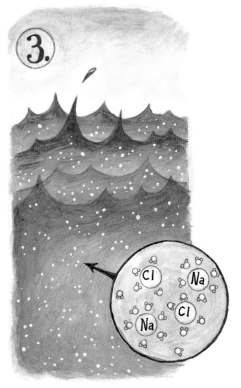

CHECK IT OUT!

If you had all the salt in the ocean on top of a dried-out Earth, you could cover the whole planet with a layer of salt 50 meters (half a soccer field) thick.

Estuaries [Ess-(tch)yoo-AIR-eez]—Where Freshwater Rivers Meet Saltwater Oceans

As you might figure, the water there is not as salty as the rest of the ocean, and not as fresh as a running river. Water flowing through estuaries is always mixing nutrients into the soil and the sea. That makes big food webs and busy ecosystems with lots of plants, frogs, birds, and fish.

Freshwater works its way through cells in living things (like you and me) toward saltier water. Freshwater fish have body fluids that are a little saltier than the water they swim in. Freshwater works its way through their skin, and they constantly have to pump water out of their cells and out of their bodies to avoid bloating up and dying. Saltwater fish have the opposite problem. The water around them is saltier than the water in their bodies. Water tends to naturally flow out of their bodies and into the ocean. Saltwater fish gulp seawater all the time to replace the water they lose.

TRY THIS!

THE QUESTION:
How does salt get into the ocean?

HERE'S WHAT YOU NEED:
salt • water • paper towels • a measuring cup

1 Mix a spoonful of salt into 50 ml of water.

2 Pour the saltwater onto three paper towels layered on a plate.

3 Set the plate someplace sunny and warm. Wait a few days.

What happened to the water? Where's the salt? Do you think clouds that form over the ocean have salt in them? Hmmm.

Amazing Ocean Currents

The world's oceans are always moving, carrying food and nutrients from one part to another. Ocean water masses move in "currents." Currents are the key to life in the sea. A current is like a giant river in the sea, and acts like an air pump bubbling oxygen into an aquarium.

Most public aquariums are built near large bodies of water—bays, sounds, or right on the ocean. To make a place like that work takes a huge flow of water. The Seattle Aquarium pumps 11,000 tons (!) of seawater through its tanks every day. It has a human-made current.

Where's that rubber duck?

The Peru Current. Flowing northward along the coast of South America, this river in the ocean is cold because its waters come up from the deepest, coldest layers of the ocean. It carries minerals from the ocean floor to the surface, which provide nutrients for huge "plumes" of plankton, which in turn provide food for billions of fish. As South American fishermen know, the Peru current has created one of the richest fishing grounds in the world.

CHECK IT OUT!

In 1992, a ship bound from Hong Kong got stuck in a violent Pacific Ocean storm. One of the containers on the ship split open, spilling 7,220 yellow rubber ducks overboard, as well as blue turtles, green frogs, and red beaver bath toys. Many of the toys turned up in Alaska a year later. Some of them got stuck in the ice near the North Pole. Eventually, they slid into the Atlantic Ocean on the other side of the world! At first, they were just another ton of sea trash, but soon scientists realized they could use them to study a few huge ocean currents.

Tides Come from Outer Space

Gravity makes tides in the ocean. The Earth's gravity holds the ocean on the planet. The pull of the Moon and the pull of the Sun make the ocean bulge out a little bit toward outer space. As the Earth turns, the shores of continents and islands pass through the bulges. The level of the ocean goes up and down during the day. When you're in a bulge, it's high tide. When you're on the side next to a bulge, it's low tide.

Sun

Earth

Moon

Spring Tide

Neap Tide

When the Moon or the Sun pulls a bulge in the ocean on one side of the Earth, a bulge forms in the ocean on the other side of the Earth as well. The combination of the mass of the Earth with its ocean stays in balance. (So there are two high and low tides about every day.) The amount that the Earth moves in space because of the bulges is very, very small. But, it's enough to create whole ecosystems that are like nowhere else on the land or in the sea.

Highs and Lows. When the Moon and the Sun are lined up, the tides are the highest. They're called spring tides. When they're at right angles, the tides are the lowest—neap tides. One more thing—the Moon doesn't orbit the Earth right above the equator. Its orbit is tilted, so the Earth's highest and lowest tides each day are usually on opposite sides of the equator.

Spring Tide

Neap Tide

Now that's wild!

We Are Now Entering . . . the Tidal Zone

The tidal zone is where it's wet part of the time and dry part of the time. It's an unusual place to live. Plants and animals have to be able to live underwater half the time and out of water half the time. When the tide goes out, some animals, like hermit crabs, retreat to tide pools, puddles where the seawater collects. Certain creatures, like the tiny mole crab, burrow down into the damp sand and wait for the tide to come back in. Other animals, like barnacles and limpets, seal themselves inside their shells until the water returns. At low tide, the shoreline becomes a supermarket for birds. They swoop in to find food that's not underwater.

The biggest tides we know of occur in the Bay of Fundy, in the Canadian province of Nova Scotia. The level of the ocean changes as much as 17 meters (57 feet) between low and high tide. That's a tide as high as two houses!

TRY THIS!

Where does the water go at low tide?

HERE'S WHAT YOU NEED:

a long baking dish • an empty cardboard tube • tape
a plastic drinking straw • water • blue food coloring
big felt-tip marker • scissors

1. Get a long baking dish (like the kind you make brownies in).

2. Tape an empty toilet paper tube (or half an empty paper towel tube) to the side of the dish at one end.

3. Cut the straw so that it is about as long as the pan is deep. Tape it in the corner where you can see it through the tube.

4. Fill the pan with water, and add a couple drops of blue food coloring.

5. Mark the water level on the straw with the felt-tip pen.

6. Tip the pan to one side and prop it up with a pencil or the marker. Then, mark the water level on the straw. Tip it the other way, and mark the level again. Now look through the tube. The water level changes, but it never leaves the dish—or the Earth!

Cool!

35

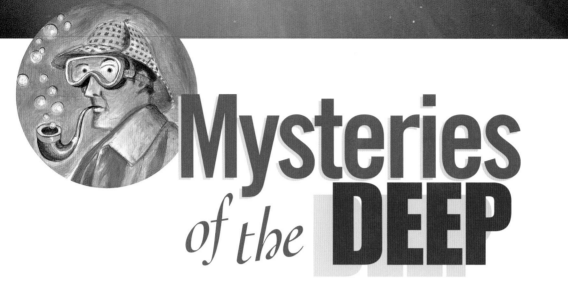

Mysteries *of the* DEEP

We call the top layer of the ocean "the photic zone"—the layer of the ocean where sunlight penetrates. How deep sunlight gets depends on how brightly the Sun is shining and how clear the water is. Usually it's 50 to 150 meters down. Ocean plants—whether seaweed or phytoplankton—need sunlight to survive. Almost all sea plants live in the photic zone.

Deep below the surface of the ocean is where the Sun just doesn't shine. Seawater soaks up the light, so there's no photosynthesis. The sea cucumbers, plume worms, and other creatures that live on the ocean floor can eat plants and animals and dead stuff that sinks from the surface. On the other hand, most deep-sea fish are predators. They hunt each other in complete darkness. That might sound difficult at first, like a bunch of people wearing blindfolds playing hide-and-seek. But the animals of the deep sea have evolved in some pretty cool ways to live without light from above.

Lights Please. Things that live in the deep ocean make their own light. A green glow can attract other animals to meet or to eat. Showing a bright light suddenly can dazzle and confuse an attacker. Some swimming animals use an array of glowing patches for camouflage. When a predator looks up from below into the background of sunlight or moonlight, the shifting patterns of light are hard to home in on.

CHECK IT

OUT!

JAWS! Megamouth sharks and gulper eels, for example, have HUGE, HUGE jaws and mouths as wide as half their length. They have lips that glow, and they scoop food day and night in the pitch dark.

Hydrothermal Vents

Scientists exploring the ocean floor discovered hydrothermal vents, cracks in the ocean floor that continually release boiling hot water from deep in the Earth's crust. Living things around hydrothermal vents don't depend directly on the Sun. Bacteria—tiny organisms—eat chemicals in the hot water to create oxygen. Small filter-feeding animals eat the bacteria, and larger animals eat the smaller animals. We end up with giant clams, mussels, and eerie red-frilled tube worms 3 meters (10 feet) long living in very hot water as far as you can get from the Sun (without drilling into the Earth!).

CHECK IT **OUT!**

The oceans are deeper than the land is high. The deepest part of the ocean—a crack in the ocean floor near the Philippines called the Challenger Deep—lies 11 kilometers (7 miles) beneath the surface of the water. If you could put Mount Everest into the Challenger Deep, the top of the mountain would still be covered by 2 kilometers (over a mile) of water. *Whoa!*

TRY THIS!

THE QUESTION:
How does the Sun affect the ocean?

HERE'S WHAT YOU NEED:
tall glass pitcher • water • food coloring • flashlight

1 Put some water in a clear, tall glass or in a glass pitcher.

2 Add a few drops of blue food coloring and mix it up.

3 Look at a flashlight shining through the side of the glass.

4 Now hold the glass over your head.

Shine the flashlight through the side of the glass, and notice how bright it looks. Now shine the light through the top of the glass and look up from the bottom. The light looks dimmer, because it's passing through more water—the light's getting soaked up. The deeper you go in the ocean, the more water there is above you to absorb light. Try it with a long, shallow baking dish.

This helps explain why you can't see the Bahamas by dipping your face in the water in Florida!

How the Earth Rocks and Rolls

Billions of years ago, the Earth started out as a big, hot ball of molten rock. Like a chocolate chip cookie, our planet cooled from the outside surface first, forming a thin, hard rocky crust. When things cool off, they shrink (except water as it turns to ice). So the crust broke off into huge plates that move and jostle each other. The plates buckle and overlap. They slowly create mountain ranges and valleys in the seafloor that are higher than the Himalayas and deeper than the Grand Canyon.

When plates move even just a little, they can cause earthquakes. There are dozens of earthquakes every day. Most of them are underwater.

Do the Wave. A tsunami [(t)soo-NAH-mee] is a huge wave that forms when the shifting, shaking seafloor lifts and shifts the water above it. Tsunamis can make giant waves. Some are measured as high as a 10-story building. They slam millions of tons of water onto the shore, which can cause terrible damage to cities on the coast of a continent.

CHECK IT OUT!

Do you know where the tallest mountain is? In the ocean! Mauna Kea, in Hawaii, reaches 10,203 meters (33,476 feet) from the seafloor to its tippy top, some 4,205 meters (13,796 feet) above sea level. By comparison, Mount Everest is only 8,848 meters (29,028 feet) tall. (Of course, that one is all above water.)

TRY THIS!

THE QUESTION:

How are tsunamis created?

HERE'S WHAT YOU NEED:

a plastic lid (like from a whipped cream or a large yogurt container)
string • duct tape • a bathtub • water • a few soda bottle caps

1 Attach a piece of string with tape to the center of the plastic lid, or poke a hole through the lid and tie the string on in a knot.

2 Fill the bathtub with just a little bit of water, so that the head of the tub is dry. You'll have a tub-wide beach.

3 Place one or a few upside-down soda bottle caps right on the water's edge. They are like the buildings on a beach.

4 Place the lid under water down at the tub's drain, where it's deepest.

5 Grab the string, and pull it up fast. You will create a wave.

If you do this a few times, you'll see that the up and down motion of the plastic lid creates sideways motion on the beach. Also, the wave starts out pretty small, but gets big at the shallow end. Real tsunamis caused by earthquakes do the same thing, only they often knock down things a lot bigger than bottle caps!

The Ocean and YOU

Humans explore the ocean by swimming with special equipment or building machines that can go underwater. We are inventing better and better ways to see the sea. We've built big sailing ships, submarines, diving suits, scuba gear, satellite cameras, and remote-controlled submersibles. We've learned a lot, but we've really only scratched the surface, uh . . . the bottom.

Brrr. A rusty ship is not hard to find, because saltwater is corrosive. Ocean exploration equipment has to be able to handle the salt and the cold. By human standards, most places in the ocean are not warm. In deep water, the ocean is barely above freezing, but in the Gulf of Mexico, it gets up to about 24 degrees Celsius (75 degrees Fahrenheit).

CHECK IT OUT!

Water is heavy; it's massive. Just try hauling a bucket of it. When you dive into a pool or the ocean, the weight of the water above you creates pressure, squeezing the air out of your lungs and crushing air-filled containers—like submarines. Things that go deep have to handle a lot of pressure.

> By the way, ice floats. That's why no matter how cold it gets, icebergs stay on the surface.

The Bends

If we breathe pressurized air for too long, extra gas, especially nitrogen, dissolves in our blood. If we go back up to low pressure too fast, dangerous bubbles can form in our bloodstream. Divers say they feel these bubbles first in their elbows and knees (where their arms and legs bend). It's very serious, and it got named "the bends."

Scuba. Jacques Cousteau and Émile Gagnan invented the self-contained underwater breathing apparatus (scuba). They realized that we humans are mostly water. You can squeeze our bodies pretty hard with pressure, and we'll be okay. So scuba equipment supplies a diver with air under pressure. It's strong enough to fill our lungs with air even though the water around us is squeezing in.

TRY THIS!

THE QUESTION:
How can divers avoid getting "the bends"?

HERE'S WHAT YOU NEED:
2 unopened bottles of soda

1 Get two unopened bottles of soda at room temperature.

2 Shake them up.

3 Now hold one of them over the sink and twist it open fast.

4 Now get the second bottle. Twist the top slowly. Stop twisting and then twist slowly again.

The bubbles in the soda are like the dangerous bubbles a diver might get in his or her joints when he or she has not come up from the deep carefully and has the bends. Divers can avoid the bends by moving up slowly, and stopping once in a while to let the bubbles wash out of their system.

People
Affect the Ocean

No matter where you go in the ocean, you will find pollution. The ocean looks huge (and it is), but it's a small world in a way. Poison from factory waste way, way inland finds its way to the sea. Oil from spills finds its way inside ocean animals as well as the humans and other animals that eat them. Would you want to eat a fish loaded with poison? Well, neither do fish. You don't have to be near the ocean to pollute it. When it rains, chemicals in fertilizers from farm fields and city garbage from landfills get carried through rivers and underground to the sea . . . see?

Not a Pretty Sight. When deep-sea exploration first became possible in the 1950s, U.S. Admiral R. J. Galanson sonar-phoned back from 11 kilometers down (7 miles deep) that he could see an empty beer can in front of him on the Pacific Ocean floor. Pollution is everywhere in the sea.

Population Explosion

Since 1900, the Earth's population has risen from about 1.5 billion to almost 6 billion humans. The level of the ocean has also risen. The Earth is kept warm by gases in our atmosphere. That's the "greenhouse effect." As more people drive cars, build factories, and use electricity (from coal and gas-burning power plants), smoggy pollution fills our skies. These gases in the air cause the greenhouse effect to get stronger than it would if we weren't burning this stuff. The world is getting warmer; the ice in the Arctic and Antarctic is melting a little, raising the level of the sea. If the Earth warms up too much, cities along the coast will just flood . . . completely.

Plastic bags aren't nutritious like good ol' mesoglea!

One Problem with Plastic. Sea turtles often confuse plastic bags with the sea jellies they like to eat, and they choke and die after eating them.

YOU Can Make a Difference!

Where do giant squid meet and mate?

Why do bacteria glow?

How much will the sea rise if the earth gets warmer?

How did animals find their way to hydrothermal vents?

How much fishing is too much fishing?

Can we farm the oceans and grow food there?

How do currents change?

Can we figure out a way to talk to whales?

By exploring and studying the ocean, we can understand our place on Earth—please see page 5. . . .

Maybe you'll be the scientist who discovers the answers to these and the tens of thousands of other questions about the ocean!

The more we know about the ocean, the better we can protect it and ourselves. Ocean scientists have lots of questions, and we need answers. The ocean affects your life, and how you live affects the ocean.

BILL NYE has won more than a dozen Daytime Emmy Awards for his hugely popular show, *Bill Nye the Science Guy®*. A recognized science expert, he has worked to improve science education in our schools and at home. He served on the President's Panel on Education and the Department of Energy Task Force on Education, and he has testified before the Federal Communications Commission about the importance of informal science education. He is also the author of *Bill Nye the Science Guy's® Great Big Dinosaur Dig* and *Bill Nye the Science Guy's® Consider the Following: A Way Cool Set of Science Questions, Answers, and Ideas to Ponder*.

JOHN S. DYKES's artwork has appeared in numerous national magazines, including *Time* and *Newsweek*. He lives with his family in Connecticut.